WHO ARE THE CHURCH?

THE PÈRE MARQUETTE
LECTURE IN THEOLOGY
2008

WHO ARE THE CHURCH?

JOSEPH A. KOMONCHAK

MARQUETTE
UNIVERSITY
PRESS

LIBRARY OF CONGRESS CATALOGING-IN-PUBLICATION DATA

Komonchak, Joseph A.
 Who are the church? / Joseph A. Komonchak.
   p. cm. — (The Père Marquette lecture in theology ; 2008)
 Includes bibliographical references.
 ISBN-13: 978-0-87462-588-2 (clothbound : alk. paper)
 ISBN-10: 0-87462-588-2 (clothbound : alk. paper)
 1. Church. I. Title.
BV600.3.K66 2008
262'.7—dc22

                                        2008001097

© 2008
Marquette University Press
Milwaukee WI 53201-3141
All rights reserved.

Manufactured in the United States of America
Member, Association of American University Presses

MARQUETTE UNIVERSITY PRESS
MILWAUKEE

The Association of Jesuit University Presses

FOREWORD

The 2008 Père Marquette Lecture in Theology is the thirty-ninth in a series commemorating the missions and explorations of Père Jacques Marquette, S.J. (1637-75). This series of lectures was begun in 1969 under the auspices of the Marquette University Department of Theology.

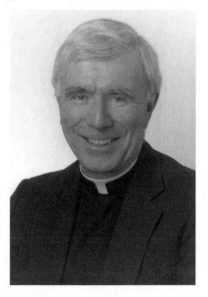

JOSEPH A. KOMONCHAK

The Joseph A. Auchter Family Endowment Fund has endowed the lecture series. Joseph Auchter (1894-1986), a native of Milwaukee, was a banking and paper industry executive and a long-time supporter of education. The fund was established by his children as a memorial to him.

The Rev. Joseph A. Komonchak was born in Nyack, New York, in 1939. He was educated at Cathedral College, New York, and at St. Joseph's Seminary, Yonkers, New York, from which he received an A.B. degree in 1960. From 1960 to 1964 he studied at the North American College and at the Pontifical Gregorian University in Rome. He was ordained a priest for the Archdiocese of New York in 1963 and earned a Licentiate in Sacred Theology at the Gregorian in 1964.

From 1964 to 1967 he served as a curate at St. Bartholomew's Church in Yonkers, N.Y., while also teaching theology at the College of New Rochelle. In 1967 he joined the theology faculty at St. Joseph's Seminary, where he taught until 1977. He received his PhD in theology at Union Theological Seminary in New York in 1976. Since 1977 he has taught theology at the Catholic University of America in Washington, D.C. He has taught courses on the Church, on ministry, on the Church's social teaching, on modern and contemporary Catholic theology, on the thought of John Courtney Murray, and on the history and theology of Vatican II.

In 1996 he was named the first occupant of the John C. and Gertrude P. Hubbard Chair in Religious Studies at the Catholic University of America.

He is the chief editor of *The New Dictionary of Theology*. A specialist in the history and theology of the Second Vatican Council, he is the editor of the English edition of the five-volume *History of Vatican II*. He is the author also of *Foundations in Ecclesiology* (Boston: Lonergan Workshop, 1995). He has published well over a hundred articles in journals such as *Concilium, Cristianiesimo nella Storia, The Journal of Religion, The Review of Politics, Revue d'Histoire Ecclésiastique, Theological Studies*, and *The Thomist*.

In the present lecture, Professor Komonchak shows why many consider him the dean of American ecclesiologists. He explores the hypothesis that for every statement one makes about the Church, one should be ready to answer the question, "Of whom am I speaking?" This takes him into the relationship between the statements made about the Church in scripture and tradition, on the one hand, and the community of sinful persons who gather as Church, on the other. He supports his own position with the authority of St. Augustine and St. Thomas Aquinas, and relates his views to those of Hans Urs von Balthasar and Avery Dulles. He draws on Bernard Lonergan's notion of constitutive meaning to answer the question, "What sort of entity is the Church?" And he displays an unfailing command of relevant texts from the Church's official teaching bodies.

Robert M. Doran, SJ

WHO ARE THE CHURCH?

JOSEPH A. KOMONCHAK

I should perhaps explain from the outset what my talk is not about. In asking, "Who are the Church?" I am not asking about relations between the clergy and the laity. Neither am I asking, "Who are the members of the Church?" at least not as that question is usually raised. Nor am I asking which claimants to the title – Protestants, say, or Orthodox, or Catholics – are "the one, true Church," although the meaning of that question will come up for discussion at the end of the essay.

What I am asking is this: Of whom is one speaking when one speaks of the Church? To whom does the word refer? Of whom is it true? *In* whom is it true?

Behind my question lies an hypothesis that I would like to explore here, namely, that with regard to every statement one makes about the Church, one should be prepared to answer those questions. This may appear to be an unexceptionable claim. But a little reflection on our own use of the term may both personalize our inquiry and alert us to the difficulty of pursuing it.

So let me begin by asking everyone here whether you would be ready to say of whom you are speaking when you use the word "Church." Yves Congar, as we will see, claimed that in the early centuries, the Church was the "*Nous* des chrétiens," the Christian "We"; it was what was meant when Christians used the first-person plural. Well, in your usual statements, is "Church" a third-person word, or a first-person word, that is, does it also refer to yourself? What first comes to mind when you hear the word "Church"? What image? What concept? When you hear some of the classic terms applied to the Church – People of God, Body of Christ, Temple of the Spirit, Bride of Christ, Mother Church – what do you take them to mean? (Do you even wonder about this?) In your mind, do they have anything to do with what you know and experience as the Church? Do they have anything to do with you? Can you point to anything in your own life, or in that of other Christians along with you, that corresponds to these statements, to which these statements might be thought to refer? What must be true of you if these terms are true of the Church? If these terms are not true of you, are they true of anyone else in the Church? After all, if they are not true of anyone in the Church, what can it mean to say that they are true of the Church?

If there is a single question that has haunted me for the forty years that I have now been teaching ecclesiology, it concerns the relationship between the glorious things that are said in the Bible and in the tradition about the Church – "*Gloriosa dicta sunt de te, civitas Dei!*" (Ps 86:3) – and the concrete community of limited and sinful men and women who gather as the Church at any time or place all around the world. The Catholic tradition, most recently at the Second Vatican Council, had insisted that the glorious things were true of the "often small and poor and scattered" communities (*Lumen gentium* 26). But, on the one hand, it seemed to me that ordinary Christians commonly did not know how to relate the glorious things to their own experience of the Church; the phrase "People of God" interested them, at least for a while, but their eyes seemed to glaze over when someone spoke of the "Mystical Body of Christ" or "Mother Church" or "Bride." Theologians might have found it interesting to explore such notions, but what could they have to do with the people in the pew?

On the other hand, ecclesiologists, especially after the Second Vatican Council, did not spend a great deal of time exploring what it meant for these communities to be called by these glorious names. Titles such as People of God, Body of Christ, Temple of the Spirit were commonly explored in such strictly theological terms, as the Scriptures, the tradition, the liturgy handed them on, that it was easy to forget that what was being talked about was a group of human beings. It was as if there is an entity, somewhere above them, a suprapersonal reality, of which these things are true, an entity that is whatever these images say it is, that does whatever they say it does, apart from concrete men and women and their communities. At perhaps the limit, this takes the form of the claim that the Church is a person, or has a personal subsistence, distinct from the persons of her members, and it is to this person that one points as the subject of the actions most distinctive and constitutive of the Church.

My title resembles that of a well-known article by Hans Urs von Balthasar, published first in 1961 and announcing many of the themes he would develop in his great trilogy: "Who is the Church?" he asked.[1] That he asked, "Who is the Church?" and not "What is the Church?" has often been pointed out; the question is personalized, in other words:

---

[1] Hans Urs von Balthsar, "Who is the Church?" in *Spouse of the Word: Explorations in Theology, II* (San Francisco: Ignatius Press, 1991) 143-91. On Balthasar's view, see Jean-Noel Dol, "Qui est l'Église? Hans Urs von Balthasar et la Personnalité de l'Église," *Nouvelle Revue Théologique* 117 (1995) 376-95; Larry S. Chapp, "Who is the Church? The Personalistic Categories of Balthasar's Ecclesiology," *Communio*, 26 (1996) 322-38. Angelo Scola follows Balthasar closely in his own work, *Chi è la Chiesa? Una chiave antropologica e sacramentale per l'ecclesiologia* (Brescia: Queriniana, 2005).

whatever "essence" of the Church is sought, it will not be found in the realm of the non-personal. This may be what he meant in the first sentence of the article: "To frame the question in this way is to presuppose that the Church is 'someone,' in other words a person." He goes on:

> A person, however, seems definable only as a spiritual center of consciousness of free and rational acts. How, then, can the Church be a person in this sense? We are, of course, wont to attribute to the Church all kinds of acts: the Church wills this and that, rejoices, suffers, permits one thing or another, commands, forbids; above all she prays, thanks, intercedes, hopes, sacrifices, and, as regards men, she instructs, admonishes, feeds them.

The question naturally arises: Who is the general subject of such statements? – by which I think he means both "Who is the subject of these sentences?" and "Who is the subject, that is, the agent of the actions mentioned?"

You will have noticed that Balthasar asked his question in the singular, "Who is the Church?" And his answer was that the Church is a person, also in the singular. He goes on to exclude as inadequate to the mystery of the Church's union with Christ an analogy drawn from collective persons such as a state or a corporation. He writes: "She is not a mere collectivity that, in comparison with the real inter-

connection between one generation and another
of mankind as a whole, always has something ficti-
tious and accidental about it." Instead, "Church"
refers to "real subjects, ... but only such as partici-
pate through divine grace in a normative subject
and its consciousness."[2] He explores the personality
of the Church particularly as the Bride of Christ,
the image that will dominate in the subsequent development of the article and, indeed, in the whole
of Balthasar's ecclesiology and perhaps even in his
total theological synthesis.[3] Real subjects, that is,
real human beings, are the Church insofar as they
share in her bridal consciousness, realized most fully
in the Blessed Virgin Mary. At the end of the essay,
he summarizes:

> We have attempted to give some intimation of
> the personality of the Church. We could not
> hypostasize the Church, nor did we wish to
> see her as a mere collectivity. Neither is there a
> collective person resulting from the merging of
> individual persons. There is absolutely no analogy
> for the reality that revelation calls the bride of
> Christ; and since God's Trinitarian consciousness
> in Christ is embedded in her to make her a bride,

[2] Balthasar, "Who is the Church?" 179.
[3] Balthasar returned to the question in the third volume
of his *Theo-Drama: Theological Dramatic Theory* (San
Francisco: Ignatius Press, 1992) 263-456.

> an individual subject, the subject-being is itself
> a mystery of faith.[4]

I have chosen to ask my question in the plural: "Who are the Church?" I do so because I wish it to be clear from beginning to end that the Church is a social phenomenon, and that any answer to the question about the referent of the word will always refer us to a group of people, to "real subjects."[5] As will become clear, I think that there is more to be gained from comparisons with other human groups than Balthasar thinks, in other words, that the uniqueness of the Church in her theological mystery does not preclude but in fact requires exploration of what she may have in common with other human communities.

RECENT DEVELOPMENTS IN ECCLESIOLOGY

Let me go on, then, to explain why I ask my question as I do by offering a very rapid survey of recent ecclesiology. Throughout the last century, a series of notions of the Church began to be proposed as alternatives to an approach to the Church that focused, sometimes almost exclusively, on her institutional

[4] Balthasar, "Who is the Church?" 186 (translation modified).
[5] Throughout this essay, I will be focusing on the Church on earth, as composed of human beings, which need not mean neglecting her, that is, their relationship to the angels and saints already in glory.

dimensions. With roots in medieval Church-State controversies and the quarrel that pitted papalists against conciliarists, the standard treatment of the Church was further elaborated in response to the various Protestant ecclesiologies and in particular to the proposed distinction between the visible Church and the invisible Church, the latter often called the "true" or "real" Church. In opposition to this view, Robert Bellarmine maintained that there is a single Church as readily identifiable as the Kingdom of France or the Republic of Venice. It is "the group of people linked by the profession of the same Christian faith and by communion in the same sacraments, under the governance of legitimate pastors and especially of the single vicar of Christ on earth, the Roman Pontiff." This approach led to very clear results: the profession of faith excluded non-believers such as Jews, Muslims, pagans, heretics and apostates; sacramental communion excluded catechumens and excommunicates; submission to authority excluded schismatics. Everyone else was included, even reprobates, scoundrels, or the impious. Indeed, the advantage of this approach, Bellarmine said, was this:

> All the other views require inner virtues to establish someone in the Church and for that reason they make the true Church invisible; whereas, even though we believe that all the virtues – faith, hope, charity, and the others – are

found in the Church, we do not think that for someone to be able to be said to be in some way part of the true Church of which the Scriptures speak any inner virtue is required, but only the external profession of the faith and sacramental communion, both of which can be perceived by the senses. For the Church is a group of people as visible and palpable as is the group of the Roman people or the Kingdom of France or the Republic of Venice. [6]

With further emphasis placed upon the teaching office of the Church in response to Enlightenment rationalism, there resulted a notion of the Church as a *societas perfecta*, that is, as a juridically independent, sovereign, and self-sufficient social body with a hierarchically articulated structure of authority. It is what Avery Dulles called "the institutional model" of the Church.[7]

[6] Robert Bellarmine, *De Controversiis*, II, Bk III, "De Ecclesia militante toto orbe terrarum diffusa" (Naples: Giuliano, 1837) 75; see Joseph A. Komonchak, "Concepts of Communion, Past and Present," *Cristianesimo nella Storia* 16 (1995) 321-40.

[7] Avery Dulles, *Models of the Church* (Garden City: Doubleday, 1972) 42. For a good summary of this approach, see also Yves Congar, "Situation ecclésiologique au moment de 'Ecclesiam suam' et passage à une Église dans l'itinéraire des hommes," in *Le Concile de Vatican II: Son Église, Peuple de Dieu et Corps du Christ* (Paris: Beauchesne, 1984) 7-32.

While richer concepts of the Church were offered by such nineteenth-century figures as Johann Adam Möhler and John Henry Newman, the institutional approach continued to prevail. Slowly, however, in the twentieth century, more theological notions of the Church began to be proposed.[8] The idea of the Church as the Mystical Body of Christ had a powerful influence on the thought and life of the Church from the 1920s to the end of the 1950s; it helped inspire numerous Catholic Action groups, for example, as well as the liturgical movement.[9] Pope Pius XII's encyclical *Mystici Corporis*

---

[8] Stanislas Jaki, *Les tendances nouvelles de l'ecclésiologie* (Rome: Herder, 1957) is still valuable; see also Antonio Acerbi, "Panorama delle tendenze giuriste e delle tendenze communionali nella ecclesiologia dal Vaticano I al Vaticano II," in *Due ecclesiologie: Ecclesiologia giuridica ed ecclesiologia di communione nella "Lumen Gentium"* (Bologna: Ed. Dehoniane, 1975) 13-105; Angel Anton, "Lo sviluppo della dottrina sulla Chiesa nella teologia dal Vaticano I al Vaticano II," in *L'ecclesiologia dal Vaticano I al Vaticano II* (Brescia: La Scuola, 1973) 27-86. For the situation on the eve of Vatican II, see Congar, "Situation ecclésiologique," and his "Peut-on définir l'Eglise? Destin et valeur de quatre notions qui s'offrent à le faire," in *Sainte Église: Études et approches ecclésiologiques* (Unam Sanctam 41; Paris: du Cerf, 1963) 21-44.

[9] The literature here is immense; for a start, see Joseph Bluett, "The Mystical Body, A Bibliography, 1890-1940," *Theological Studies* 3 (1942) 260-89; J. Eileen

(1941) was an effort to integrate one understanding of the idea with the modern institutional model. In the late 1950s the idea of the Church as the People of God was revived and played a major role at the Second Vatican Council. The Council also made use of the idea of the Church as a "sacrament," an idea that had quietly emerged at the same time as "People of God" and has since been developed from an original sacramental referent to be used as a way of articulating the Church's role in society.[10] In the last quarter century or so, the notion of the Church as communion (*koinonia*) has spread widely and been taken by some as the key to the ecclesiology of Vatican II and as providing a firm foundation of ecumenical dialogue.

It is clear that Vatican II represents the end of one development and the beginning of others. There is a paragraph in the Dogmatic Constitution on the Church, *Lumen gentium*, that gathers the several strains in ecclesiology so briefly set out above and forces on our attention the question in my title: Who are the Church? The eighth and last paragraph of the constitution's first chapter, on the mystery of the Church, had set out in succession the origins of

---

Scully, "The Theology of the Mystical Body in French Language Theology 1930-1950: A Review and Assessment," *Irish Theological Quarterly,* 58 (1992) 58-74.

[10] See Yves Congar, *Un peuple messianique: Salut et libération* (Paris: du Cerf, 1975).

the Church in the Trinity (2-4), her relationship to
the Kingdom of God announced and inaugurated
by Christ (5), the multiple biblical images of the
Church (6) with special attention given to the images of the Church as the Body of Christ and the
Bride of Christ (7). To avoid the impression that
this description is "merely idealistic and unreal,"
the chapter's final paragraph addresses the question
where this Church, just described in the great span
of the divine vision from creation to eschatological
fulfilment, "is concretely found."[11]

The first important statement is the familiar argument that there is a single Church, and to press
the point, the Council sets out, as if in parallel col-
umns, the two dimensions of the Church. Thus,
the Church is both a community of faith, hope,
and love and a visible structure; both the mystical Body of Christ and a hierarchically articulated
society; both a spiritual community and a visible
group; both endowed with heavenly gifts and existing here on earth; both holy and always in need of
purification. The formal statement is that "one is
not to think of these as two realities but as forming
a single complex reality that comes together from

[11] This is how the Council's Doctrinal Commission described the purpose of the eighth paragraph of *Lumen
gentium*; see *Acta Synodalia Sacrosancti Concilii Oe-
cumenici Vaticani II*, III/I (Typis Polyglottis Vaticanis,
1973) 176.

a divine and from a human element." Having established this crucial point, the Council goes on to answer its question as to where this Church is to be found. This single reality, it says, the Church of Christ, "constituted and organized as a society in this world subsists in the Catholic Church..., even though outside her structure many elements of sanctification and of truth are found."

The use of the verb *subsistit in*, substituted in the final text for the verb *est* (is), remains quite controversial, and I will return to the question later. Here I am more interested in the Council's insistence that the divine and the human in the Church not be separated from one another as if they referred to distinct entities. The paragraph cautiously offers a comparison with the mystery of Christ himself, both divine and human.[12] The analogy holds in this respect, that as the Scriptures make two sets of statements about Jesus of Nazareth, one set stating or implying divinity, the other stating or implying humanity, so also of an obviously quite human group of men and women statements are made in the Scriptures that relate them directly to the Trin-

[12] The caution is necessary because in the Church there is no hypostatic union between divinity and humanity; hence also the caution in speaking of the Church as "the continued incarnation"; on this see Yves Congar, "Dogme christologique et ecclésiologie: Vérité et limites d'un parallèle," in *Sainte Église* 69-104.

ity: they are the People of God, the Body of Christ, the Temple of the Holy Spirit. This in fact is what the Council meant by speaking of the Church as "mystery": it took the word in its Pauline sense to refer to "a transcendent and salvific reality which is revealed and made manifest in some visible way":[13] thus there is a mystery of divine election in Israel, there is the mystery of Christ, and there is the mystery of the Church. Remove the humanity from either Christ or the Church, and there is no mystery. Remove the divinity, and there is no mystery. Separate the two as if one set of statements apply to one reality and the other to another, and there is no mystery. One of the chief tasks of ecclesiology is to try to understand how such glorious things can be said of a group of sinful human beings.

Lumen gentium brought together several notions of the Church – communion in mystery, Body of Christ, People of God, sacrament. But after the Council it was not uncommon for people to put these notions into tension with one another, even in opposition to one another. The result was that it almost seemed that one had to choose among the various images and concepts of the Church employed by the Council. Avery Dulles's *Models*

[13] This is how the Doctrinal Commission explained what was meant by speaking of the Church as "mystery," as in the title of the first chapter of *Lumen gentium*; see *Acta Synodalia*, III/1, 170.

of the Church was at times misinterpreted as if his five models were mutually exclusive, or even as if they described, not five ways of thinking and speaking about the Church, but five ways of being the Church. Since his book was so widely read, it may be worth a moment to consider what Dulles offered in his book and to reflect on some methodological questions it raises.

What do the Models Model?

In the first chapter of his book, Fr. Dulles, agreeing with Yves Congar that a single definition of the Church is impossible,[14] proposed to follow the Scriptures, early tradition, and *Lumen gentium* and to make use instead of a variety of images or symbols of the Church. These first-order expressions, when subjected to critical and systematic second-order reflection, may yield "models" of the Church, serving both synthetic and heuristic functions insofar as they integrate a large variety of aspects of the Church and propose questions for further understanding of her complex reality. Dulles was not consistent in his distinction between these two orders of discourse, however, nor between their two distinct modes of expression, images and models. In some crucial passages, he seemed to move unconsciously from one to the other, as if all models are based upon distinctive images and as if different rules did not govern the two kinds of discourse. For

---

[14] See Yves Congar, "Peut-on définir l'Église?", cited above.

example, from the fact that, precisely because they
are so concrete, there need to be a great variety of
images of the Church, it does not follow that a great
variety of models is needed. A single model, in fact,
could recommend itself for its ability to integrate
the insights mediated by a number of images; in
fact, one could even argue that this is the goal of a
systematic theology of the Church.

But there is a more fundamental issue, which may
be pointed to by quoting from the expanded edition of *Models of the Church*. The five models Dulles
had set forth in the first edition he said were not the
product of "theological journalism"; they reflect, he
said, "the salient features of the Church of Christ
as it exists at any time or place," "the permanent
characteristics of the Church," which he then set
out very neatly:

> By its very constitution, the Church is a com-
> munion of grace (Model 2) structured as a human
> society (Model 1). While sanctifying its own
> members, it offers praise and worship to God
> (Model 3). It is permanently charged with the
> responsibility of spreading the good news of the
> gospel (Model 4) and of healing and consolidating
> the human community (Model 5).[15]

While this nicely summarizes the whole book and
helps one to understand more clearly that the mod-

[15] Avery Dulles, *Models of the Church*, expanded edition
(Garden City: Doubleday Image Books, 1987) 204.

els-approach does not in fact differ all that much from an approach by way of "aspects" or "dimensions" of the Church,[16] it is striking that this quotation, and indeed the whole book it summarizes, leaves unstated what it is that these are models of, what it is that these are features, characteristics of. The question may appear too obvious, banal even, since its answer is so obvious: they are efforts to understand *the Church*! It is as if everyone knows what is meant by "the Church," as if the object of ecclesiology is so obvious that it does not need to be stated.[17] It may also be that Dulles wanted to make the point that the Church is what one will have understood by understanding the models and placing them into relationship with one another, so that

[16] In the first edition of *Models of the Church*, p. 8-9, Dulles had said, on the one hand, that each model "calls attention to certain aspects of the Church that are less clearly brought out by the other models," and, on the other hand, that "the peculiarity of models, as contrasted with aspects, is that we cannot integrate them into a single synthetic vision on the level of articulate, categorical thought. In order to do justice to the various aspects of the Church, as a complex reality, we must work simultaneously with different models." I believe that this sets the theological sights too low.

[17] The complexities of stating and defining the object of ecclesiology are well set out in the first two chapters of Severino Dianich, *Ecclesiologia: Questioni di metodo et una proposta* (Cinisello Balsamo: Ed. Paoline, 1993).

to start off with a notion of the Church is to beg
the question. In other words, he may have felt that
to answer the question "Who is the Church?" one
must already be making use of a particular model,
and that the answer to the question will differ with
each distinct model.

But is this in fact true? Take the first-order images
and symbols, of which there are so many. In his
book on the subject Paul Minear claimed to find
ninety-six images of the Church in the New Testament, and to them could be added a great many
more found in the writings of the Fathers of the
Church, in hymns, and liturgical rites.[18] How does
one know that these very diverse images refer to the
Church? How does one know that a field in which
both wheat and weeds grow is a net dragging in
fish both good and bad, is a boat, is a little flock,
is a building, is a bride, is a mother, etc.? Few of
these are explicitly referred to the Church, but the
case can be made that they all refer to the Church.
Must one not have some at least heuristic notion
of the Church in order to be able to say that these
symbols refer to the same reality? If so, what is the
reality to which they point? Or better, to approach

[18] Paul Minear, *Images of the Church in the New Testament*
(Philadelphia, Westminster Press, 1960); Hugo Rahner,
Symbole der Kirche: Die Ekklesiologie der Väter (Salzburg:
Otto Müller 1964).

my question, Who are they to whom these images and symbols point?

If one turns to the second-order reflections articulated as models, the same question can be asked. If these are models of the same reality, one must have some notion of that reality that transcends the different theories. Is it a notion of people, of human beings? If so, who are the Church that may be thought of as an institution, a mystical communion, a sacrament, a herald, a servant? Are the same persons intended when one speaks of the Church in terms of each of these and other possible models? Of whom are these statements true? In whom are they true? And what does it mean to say that they are true of them and in them? What must be true of the Church's members if these things are true of the Church? Can they be true of the Church if they are not true of the Church's members? Must this mean: true of all the Church's members? Or is it enough that it be true of some of them?

The late Italian theologian Giuseppe Colombo asked similar questions when commenting on Dulles's method. Noting that the questions may appear banal, he replied that "in the context of post-conciliar ecclesiology, which is often rather rhetorical, the question's very banality can play a demythologizing role and help clarify things. In particular, raising the topic of its referent prevents ecclesiological reflection from being dispersed, impels it toward unity, and clarifies its meaning."[19] By the "rhetorical" character of much ecclesiology since the Council I suspect that Colombo meant the fact that elaborations of the notions of the Church that have vied for attention – Mystical Body, People of God, *koinonia*, sacrament, Bride of Christ, etc. – are often almost exclusively concerned with their theological and spiritual meaning, with comparatively little attention to their realization in concrete human beings and in concrete communities. Where this happens, ecclesiology fails to meet the task set by *Lumen gentium* when it insisted on the inseparability of the divine and the human, the spiritual and the institutional, in the actual Church.

A Way out of the Dilemma?

Some years later, Dulles offered, perhaps unintentionally, an answer to the question being asked when he proposed a sixth model, the Church as "a community of disciples," a phrase that he borrowed from Pope John Paul II's first encyclical, *Redemptor hominis*, #21.[20] Whereas in the first edition of *Mod-*

[19] Giuseppe Colombo, "'Popolo di Dio' e 'mistero' della Chiesa nell'ecclesiologia post-conciliare," *Teologia*, 10 (1985) 97-169, at 148-51.

[20] The notion was first set out in an essay, "Imaging the Church for the 1980s," *Thought* 56 (June 1981) 121-38, and then included in *A Church to Believe In: Discipleship and the Dynamics of Freedom* (New York: Crossroad,

els of the Church, Dulles had clearly preferred the sacrament model to the others, now his preference fell upon this new model which he spoke of as one that could retrieve what was valuable in the other five models. In fact, one might even be tempted to see it as a "super-model" since Dulles at first said that it can "save what is valid in these other models, while avoiding what is misleading or questionable." When he adapted this essay and included it in an expanded edition of the book, however, he repeated his view that "there can be no supermodel that does full justice to all aspects of the Church." Still, he thought that the discipleship-model might "harmonize the differences" among the other models; calling it "a variant of the communion model," he thought it "builds bridges to the other four models" and "without being adequate to the full reality of the Church," it had "potentialities as a basis for a comprehensive ecclesiology." After exploring the meaning of the phrase, he ended by indicating his belief that it had advantages over the sacramental model he had earlier preferred and took pains to answer objections to it. This was not enough, however, to make him think that it is any more than "one perspective on the Church," needing to be supplemented by the other models.

1982) 1-18; it appeared in adapted form in *Models of the Church*, expanded edition (Garden City: Doubleday Image Books, 1987) 204-26.

I hope that Cardinal Dulles will forgive me for saying that I do not think he has grasped the precise significance of his sixth model and the role it can play as a bridge among models. I believe that in fact it is not a new model at all, but that it serves to answer the question that Colombo and I have posed: it tells us who it is that the first-order images are describing, who it is to whom the second-order models refer. It identifies, in other words, the subject of ecclesiology: the Church is the community of disciples of Jesus Christ. "Community of disciples" serves to designate what it is that is said to be, say, the People of God, the Body of Christ, the Temple of the Holy Spirit, what it is that is proposed for critical and systematic understanding when it is set forth as an institution, *communio*, sacrament, herald, servant. It is not so much a sixth model, in other words, as a pointer to that to which images and models of the Church are referring when they are said to refer to something called "the Church." It is this common referent of all language and discourse about the Church that, as Colombo noted, keeps ecclesiology from drifting off into a rhetorical theological empyrean and from dispersal into an unreconciled variety of approaches and theories.

As Dulles noted, in several New Testament texts, "disciples" is virtually synonymous with "Christians" or "believers."[21] The phrase "community of disciples," then, approximates one of the oldest and most common terms for the Church, "*congregatio* (or *convocatio*) *fidelium*," the assembly of believers. I believe that this is more than a nominal definition of the Church, an identification of that to which the word refers. It approximates a real definition, that is, a statement of what constitutes and distinguishes the gathering of human beings known as the Church. It is a primary notion, both sociologically and theologically. Sociologically, it can build upon theories of community as constituted by shared experiences, shared understandings and judgments, and shared values. These common meanings and values constitute the *fides*, the commitment of mind and heart that defines and distinguishes these believers.

Theologically, "*congregatio fidelium*" is a primary notion because in the genesis of the Church nothing except the word and grace of God is prior to faith. Faith is the *humanae salutis initium*, the beginning of our salvation, said the Council of Trent (DS 1532). For St. Augustine faith marked the beginning of the Church on a journey that ends only in the blessed sight of God; it was the beginning of our betrothal to Christ that will be consummated

---

[21] Dulles, *Models of the Church*, expanded edition, p. 211.

in marriage in the Kingdom.[22] In the Decree on the
Ministry and Life of Presbyters, the Second Vatican
Council said that "the People of God is first gathered together by the Word of God" and that it is
by faith that "the *congregatio fidelium* begins and
grows" (*Presbyterorum Ordinis* 4).[23] All of the sacraments, but especially baptism and the eucharist,
are "sacraments of faith," that is, presuppose faith
in the minister and in the recipients, express faith,
foster faith.

This is, then, the referent of the word "Church"
and of any images, symbols, models that may be
employed in reference to the Church: they refer to
the assembly or community of believers, whether
gathered in particular places, or considered in their
totality as the one worldwide Church. To say that
the Church is the Mystical Body of Christ is to say
that the assembly of believers is the Mystical Body
of Christ; if the Church is the Bride of Christ, the
assembly of believers is the Bride of Christ; if the
Church is a sacrament, it is the assembly of believers that is "the sign and instrument of intimate
union with God and of the unity of the whole hu-

[22] "Ostium enim portae initium fidei unde incipit Ecclesia, et pervenit usque ad speciem: ut cum credit ea quae
non videt, mereatur perfrui cum facie ad faciem videre
coeperit." *En. in Ps. 33*, sermon 2, 2; PL 36, 308. "Ideo
et desponsata, quia desponsationis initium fides est." *Sermon 105*, 4.5; PL 38, 620.

man race" (*Lumen gentium* 1); what may be a tiny
flock of believers is for the whole human race "a
most sure seed of unity, hope and salvation" (*Lumen
gentium* 9).

These things are not said exclusively about any
single local Church, of course. They are true of other local Churches also, and true of the one catholic
Church which consists of the many local Churches,
which *is* the communion of the local Churches.
They are true, too, of the Church considered in
its totality across the span of history from creation
until the return of Christ.[24] But I wish to restrict
myself to the Church on earth and in our own generation, and in addressing the question, "Who are
the Church?", find a first answer in the statement

[23] This is why both for bishops in *Lumen gentium* 25 and
for presbyters in *Presbyterorum Ordinis* 4, the description
of the three chief tasks of the ordained ministers begins
with that of preaching.

[24] St. Augustine: "The Church that is the house of God
is also a city, for the house of God is the people of God,
the house of God is the temple of God. And what did
the Apostle say: 'God's temple is holy, which you your-
selves are' (1 Cor 3:17). All believers,... not only those
who now exist, but also those who lived before us and
those who will come after us, who are yet to be born
until the end of the world, countless believers gathered
into one,...; the whole number of holy believers..., all of
them together form the house of God and a single city,
Jerusalem herself." *En. in Ps. 126*, 4; PL 37:1669.

that the Church is the assembly, body, community, of believers in Jesus Christ.

What Sort of Entity is the Church?

To keep the discussion as concrete as I believe is necessary, I want now to talk about the genesis of the Church, that is, how the Church comes to be. I begin at a very elementary level and ask, What kind of entity is the Church? A first answer is that it is an entity in what Bernard Lonergan calls the world constituted by meaning and motivated by value.[25] It does not, that is, belong among the merely physical entities in the world, like Mt. Everest whose reality is mediated to the great majority of us by the reports of others but which itself is made up simply of rock and ice and snow. There are other entities in the world, however, that do not exist apart from human acts of meaning and value; one may think, for example, of friendships and marriages, of communities and committees, of universities and governments. Apart from acts of collective intentionality, these entities do not exist; their ontology is subjective and intersubjective.[26] One may think

[25] The notion recurs throughout Lonergan's *Method in Theology* (New York: Herder and Herder, 1972).

[26] See John Searle, *The Construction of Social Reality* (New York: Free Press, 1995), who speaks of the "co-intentionalities," that is, shared intentionalities, that bring social realities into existence and sustain them.

of community, for example, which, on Lonergan's analysis, begins and ends where common experience, common understanding, common judgments, and common decisions begin and end. The Church is one of those entities of which common meaning and value are constitutive.

As with other social entities, the constitutive dependence of the Church on acts of common meaning can be overlooked, a phenomenon sometimes known as "reification," which I am taking here in the sense defined by Peter Berger and Thomas Luckmann: "the apprehension of the products of human activity *as if* they were something else than human products – such as facts of nature, results of cosmic laws, or manifestations of divine will."[27] The temptation to reify is perhaps unavoidable since we human beings are born into a world which in its massive objectivity stands over and against us not only with its rocks and trees and cats and dogs, but also with its mothers and fathers who belong to families within communities and societies speaking a language, occupying roles within institutions, etc. – all that social and cultural fabric that is another maternal womb, as St. Augustine long ago noted,[28]

---

[27] Peter Berger and Thomas Luckman, *The Social Construction of Reality* (Garden City, NY: Doubleday Anchor Books, 1967) 89.

[28] "*Quoniam tu possedisti renes meos, Domine; suscepisti me ex utero matris meae. Dum essem in utero matris meae,*

and which, as he also noted, has at first, and even lastingly, an overwhelmingly powerful effect upon us.[29] Only later do we perhaps discover that this whole fabric was knit together by generations before us and is being sustained or altered by the gen-

---

non indifferenter habebam tenebras illius noctis et lucem illius noctis. Etenim uterus matris meae, consuetudo civitatis meae fuit." Augustine, *En. in Ps. 138*, 18; PL 37, 1795.

[29] "What does this mean: 'The words of sinners had power over us, but you will pardon our impieties'? Since we were born on this earth, we encountered sinful people and listened as they talked. If I may explain what I mean, let your attention help me, beloved. Every human being, wherever he is born, learns the language of that country or area or city and is imbued with its custom and way of life. How could a child born among pagans not worship a stone when his parents have introduced him to that worship? It was from them that he heard his first words; it was that error that he drank in with his mother's milk; and because they who were speaking were adults, while the one who was learning to speak was an infant, what could the little one do except follow the authority of his elders and consider that to be good which they were praising? Thus when the nations were later converted to Christ, and remembered the impiety of their parents, they could say what the prophet Jeremiah had already said: "Truly our parents worshipped a lie, an empty thing that could not help them" (Jer 16:19); Augustine, *En. in Ps. 64*, 6; PL 36, c. 776-77.

eration now living as we constitute the social and cultural world into which a new generation will be or is being born.

In the case of the Church the temptation to reify is particularly strong because for Christian believers the Church is indeed one of those things mentioned by Berger and Luckmann, a "manifestation of divine will." Did not Christ promise that he would build his Church on the rock of Peter (Mt 16:16)? Is the Church not called God's People? Christ's Body? the Spirit's temple? The answer to all those questions, of course, is Yes, the Church exists in virtue of God's will. One could derive from the texts of the Second Vatican Council a set of what I have elsewhere called the divine principles of the Church's constitution: the call of God, the word of Christ, the grace of the Spirit, along with the four pillars of the Church they make possible: an apostolic rule of faith, canon of Scripture, set of sacraments, and structure of ministry, all of which exist in the Church, to use the technical term, *de iure divino*, by divine right. Whatever a critique of reification in ecclesiology might mean, it cannot mean eliminating or even downplaying the divine initiative in the constitution and life of the Church.

But something like reification is a danger when the divine initiative is so stressed that what the members of the Church contribute to the realization of the Church is overlooked. The divine ele-

ments make the Church, bring her into existence,
of course; but they do so only as received in and by
the freedom of the members of the Church. The
human response to the divine initiative in word and
grace is itself a constitutive element of the Church.
What God wills to exist when he wills the Church
is a human community, a community of people,
whose constitutive meaning and value are the
common human acts of faith, hope, and love; the
Church is men and women become a community
by virtue of their co-intentionalities, whose co-in-
tentionality *is* their community. It is the common
faith, the common hope, the common love that
make this divinely willed community actually exist
– a Church with one soul because the many souls
that comprise it believe, hope, and love the same
things, the same God, the same Lord.[30] By the word

[30] " *The believers*, it says, *were one soul and one heart.* There
were many souls, but their faith made them one. There
were so many thousands of souls; they loved one another, and the many became one; they loved God in the
fire of love, and from being a multitude they came to
be the unity of beauty. If love made so many souls one
soul, what love must there be in God, where there is no
diversity but total equality?"Augustine, *De symbolo sermo
ad catechumenos*, 5; PL 40, 629. See also his marvelous
comparison of the Church to a group of people eagerly
rushing toward a shrine: "They talk to one another, and
individually set on fire, they make a single flame [*incensi
singillatim faciunt unam flammam*], and the flame cre-

and grace of God we are introduced into a share in
the divine life itself, a share in the life of the Risen
Lord so intimate and real that we can be called his
very Body; but this is, as *Lumen gentium* reminds
us, the unfathomable depth precisely of a human
community. All of the initiative lies with God, out
of his freedom; but what this free initiative enables
and effects is the liberation of our freedom by the
common love, hope, and faith that constitute and
distinguish the Church. The ontological reality of
the Church consists of the common intentional acts
of meaning and value of her members. The Church
is an event of intersubjectivity.

Consider the genesis of the Church. The Italian
theologian Severino Dianich has made the event of
ecclesiogenesis the key for a comprehensive and in-
tegrated ecclesiology.[31] He means by ecclesiogenesis
the event of communication that originally gave rise

---

ated by their conversation as they approach carries them
on to the holy place, and their holy thoughts make them
holy." *En. in Ps. 121*, 2-4; PL 37:1619.

[31] After several early essays and his programmatic statement, *Ecclesiologia: Questioni di metodo e una proposta*,
Dianich, along with Serena Noceti, elaborated a complete treatise, *Trattato sulla Chiesa* (Brescia: Queriniana,
2002). For an analysis of his work, see *Sui problemi del
metodo in ecclesiologia: In dialogo con Severino Dianich*,
ed. Antonio Barruffo (Cinisello Balsamo, Ed. San Pao-
log, 2003).

to the Church and that continues to give rise to it in every generation, indeed every day. This originating and ever-necessary event is the announcement of the death and resurrection of Jesus Christ for the salvation of the human race and the acceptance of that announcement in faith. The first four verses of the First Epistle of St. John embody this event:

> What was from the beginning, what we have heard, what we have seen with our own eyes, what we have looked upon and our hands have touched, about the word of life – for the life was made manifest, and we have seen and bear witness and announce to you the eternal life that was with the Father and has appeared to us – what we have seen and heard we announce to you also so that you may have fellowship with us, and our fellowship is with the Father and with his Son Jesus Christ. And we are writing these things so that our joy may be fulfilled (1 Jn 1:1-4).

It was belief that eternal life had appeared in Jesus of Nazareth, the one who was crucified, the one who was raised from the dead and made Messiah and Lord, that set the disciples of Jesus apart from other Jews in the days, months, and years after his earthly existence. They had seen and heard something, experienced something; and it was a word that gave them a new life, that generated a new fellowship, a *koinonia*, both horizontal (among themselves) and vertical (with God and with his Son). This communion in Christ was the sole historical difference that Jesus had made; the emergence of the Church was part of the event of Christ himself.[32] Their joy in this communion could not be complete unless they shared it with others, and so they began to preach to their fellow Jews and eventually to the Gentile world as well so that the new *koinonia* could embrace ever new members sharing that life and that joy.

It was by the communication of this message of eternal life and its reception in faith and love by successive generations that the Church continued to exist until that communication was made to our generation also; and because people have received it with faith, there continues to be a Church today.

[32] "The only difference between the world as it was just after the event [of Christ] and the world as it had been just before is that the church was now in existence. A new kind of human community had emerged; a new society had come into being. There was absolutely nothing besides. This new community held and prized vivid memories of the event in which it had begun. It had a new faith; that is, it saw the nature of the world and of God in a new light. It found in its own life the grounds – indeed anticipatory fulfilments – of a magnificent hope. But the memory, the faith, and the hope were all its own; they had neither existence nor ground outside the community. Only the church really existed. Except for the church the event had not occurred." John Knox, *The Early Church and the Coming Great Church* (London: Epworth Press, 1957) 45.

It is important to take this point in its full concreteness. The Church is born when people come to
believe in Jesus Christ;[33] she grows as more people
come to believe; she declines as fewer people continue to believe; and she ceases to exist when no
one believes the word of life. Faith is the foundation whose strength determines the strength of the
Church, St. Thomas Aquinas said.[34] There are places in the world where there were once Churches,
that is, communities of believers, but where there
are now no Churches because there are no believers. Christ's promise that the gates of hell will not
prevail against his Church is not a promise that any

[33] For all its communal dimension, "it is not possible to
think about the Church, whether theologically or his-
torically, while prescinding from what happens in the individual consciousness of a person who freely welcomes
the announcement and decides for faith. That the members of the Church are people who have freely decided to
believe is not a prior or marginal condition with respect
to the nature of the Church, but rather its basic constitu-
ent." Dianich, *Ecclesiologia*, 73-74.

[34] Thomas Aquinas, *Commentary on Colossians*, ch. 1, 1.5
(Marietti n. 57): "Fides est sicut fundamentum ex cuius
firmitate tota firmatur ecclesiae structura." The claim is
a good test case of how we think of the Church. Do
we understand it in the third person: "the Church is as
strong as her faith," thinking of it as true of something
apart from us? Have we heard it in the first person: the
Church is as strong as our faith?

single Church, any single prelate, any single Christian will prevail; in fact, any one of them can fail – did not Christ wonder whether the Son of Man, when he comes, would find faith on the earth (Lk 18:8)? What is promised is that there will always be a Church that is true to him, even if it is reduced once again to the *pusillus grex*, the insignificant flock, it once was (Lk 12:32), reduced, say, to a tiny Christian island in a vast Muslim sea.[35]

Wherever the Church arises, then, she arises out of this event of communication. She is both the process of communication and the result of the communication. This is what underlay Bernard Lonergan's description of the process by which the Church comes to exist as "the community that results from the outer communication of Christ's message and from the inner gift of God's love":

> Through communication there is constituted community and, conversely, community constitutes and perfects itself through communication. Accordingly, the Christian church is a process of self-constitution, a *Selbstvollzug* … The substance

[35] See on this concrete meaning of indefectibility, Louis Bouyer, *The Church of God: Body of Christ and Temple of the Spirit* (Chicago: Franciscan Herald Press, 1982) 496-98. St. Augustine had no difficulty in imagining such a "famine of the word" (see Amos 8:11) that only a very few true believers would remain; see *En. in Ps. 7*, 7; PL 36, 101.

> of that process is the Christian message conjoined
> with the inner gift of God's love and resulting
> in Christian witness, Christian fellowship, and
> Christian service to mankind.[36]

In more metaphorical language, this process is
what St. Bede meant when he said that "every day
the Church gives birth to the Church."[37] These are
the two aspects of the Church that Henri de Lubac
distinguished, the *Ecclesia convocans* and the *Ecclesia convocata*, that Yves Congar called the Church
as institution of salvation and the Church as the
realized community of believers.[38]

The danger must be avoided, however, of thinking that these two dimensions of the Church can
be separated, a temptation particularly acute when
the first of them (the *Ecclesia convocans*: the *Heilsanstalt*) is identified with the hierarchy, as if the laity have no role in it and as if it the clergy are not
first of all believers. The primary bearer of the word
of life from generation to generation is the whole

[36] Lonergan, *Method in Theology* 361-63. I have explored
the fruitfulness of this notion of the Church for contemporary ecclesiology in "Lonergan and Post-conciliar
Ecclesiology," to appear soon in *Lonergan Workshop*.

[37] Bede, *Explanatio Apocalypsis*, 41; PL 93, 166.

[38] Henri de Lubac, *The Splendour of the Church* (New
York: Sheed and Ward, 1956) 55-86; Yves Congar, *Vrai
et fausse réforme dans l'Église* (Paris: du Cerf,) 89-99; *Lay
People in the Church* (Westminster, MD: Newman Press,
1965) 29-58.

Church, and the ordained ministry exists, St. Paul said, in order to "equip the saints," that is, the whole body of the faithful, "for a work of ministry" (Eph 4:12). The Church bears the word of life to a new generation first of all by living by that word. The word of life is not just a word about life, that is, a teaching, but a word that gives life, so that what the Church hands on (tradition), as the Council said, is not only what she believes but also what she is.[39] At any time it is the Church already called together that is communicating the word of life and calling the Church into existence; the Church that is now doing the communicating is the Church that has resulted from the communicating. The communication can take a thousand different forms: missionary evangelization, liturgical preaching, catechetical instruction, formal Church teaching are only the more official ways of communicating. But there are also: parents speaking about God and Christ to their children; the Christian witness given daily by individuals and groups; the corporal and spiritual works of mercy; forgiveness; the witness of beauty in art, architecture, music; martyrdom – so many different ways of being not only teachers but witnesses to the vital truth we have found in Christ.

[39] See Vatican II's Dogmatic Constitution on Divine Revelation, *Dei verbum*, #8, for this notion of tradition as the handing on not only of a teaching but of a reality, life in Christ.

One might attempt a brief spiritual autobiography
and ask, Who was it who first spoke to you of God
or Christ? Who was it who helped you to take it
seriously as an adult? Was it one person in particular? A group? A parish? How did they do that? By a
word? By example? By a book? How did the word
of life come to you? Into whose human fellowship
did you enter when you came to believe?

AN ANCIENT METAPHOR

The ancient metaphor for this role of communicating the word of life is the *Ecclesia Mater*, the Church
as Mother. The image, no doubt for a variety of reasons, seems to have fallen out of favor; at least one
does not hear it very much any more. I would like
to revive it, at least for the purposes of this lecture,
in its original meaning and referent. To do so I may
have to overcome a difficulty.

Yves Congar maintained that the great turning-
point in the history of ecclesiology occurred around
the eleventh century when the need to secure and
defend the freedom of the Church against secular
rulers led churchmen, theologians, and canonists
to speak about the Church primarily in juridical
terms instead of the primarily spiritual and anthropological terms that had characterized ecclesiology
for the first millennium of Christian history. Often
enough terms that once referred to spiritual and
anthropological realities began to be given juridi-

cal significance. "Mother Church" was one of the terms that suffered this transformation. It became a term of authority, referring in particular to a suprapersonal institution that mediates salvation, gives birth to the faithful as her children whom she closely watches and warns as *mater et magistra*.[40] When I ask people what comes to mind when they hear the phrase "Holy Mother the Church," they almost always reply: the hierarchy; Rome; the Vatican... What ought to be a metaphor of affection is for many people an alienating image.

Originally, however, the motherhood metaphor applied to the whole Church and to all of her members, and it had immediate and concrete reference: it was an image for the part all could play in bringing people to birth in Christ, even in bringing Christ to birth in them, and in nurturing this new life within them. The original understanding of the metaphor was dialectical: as St. Augustine put it, "The Church is to herself both a mother and her children; for all of those of whom the Church consists, taken together, are called a mother, while those same individuals,

---

[40] Charles Journet in the first volume of what was planned as an integral ecclesiology that would do justice to the spiritual dimensions of the Church, nonetheless followed Scheeben in identifying the motherhood of the Church with the actions of the hierarchy; see *The Church of the Word Incarnate, Vol. I: The Apostolic Hierarchy* (New York: Sheed and Ward, 1956) 93-95.

taken singly, are called her children." "We are called
children of that mother," he wrote in another place,
"even though she consists of us."[41] Both elements
were present: Augustine said that Christians have
God as their father and the Church as their mother;
Mother Church bore them in her womb, gave them
birth at baptism, nursed them with the Gospel, and
reared them into Christian maturity. But if "our
single Catholic mother gave birth to all believing
Christians spread through the world," she did so
in local Churches whose baptismal waters Augustine called the womb of the Church.[42] This mother
was not something distant, apart from them; this
mother Church consisted of those who singly are
her children, and the maternal roles were carried
out by members of the local Church, both clergy
and laity. When mothers brought their newborn in-
fants to be baptized, it was Mother Church that was
bringing them.[43] If they are too young to walk to

[41] *Quaestionum Evangeliorum Libri duo*, I, 18:1; PL 35,
1327; *De diversis quaestionibus*, 75, 2; PL 40, c. 87; see
also *ibid.*, 59, 3; PL 30, 48: "All the Christians hurrying
together to Church are said to be children rushing to
their mother, even though the one who is called mother
consists of those same children."

[42] Augustine, *Sermon 46*, 18; PL 38, 280; *Sermon 119*,
4.4; PL 38, 674: "Vulva matris, aqua Baptismatis."

[43] "Ecce video Ecclesiam matrem testimonium redden-
tem ipsis uberibus suis. Accurrunt matres cum parvulis

the Church, Augustine said, "Mother Church provides them with the feet of others so they can come, with the heart of others so they can believe, with the tongue of others so they can confess the faith."[44] Congar devoted one of his most passionate writings to explaining the variety of activities this maternal role covered in the early centuries and how it could inspire an integral ecclesiology today.[45]

It may be noted in passing that St. Augustine made use of the same concrete dialectic in interpreting other images of the Church. Thus the Church was a house that Christians entered, but they themselves

---

filiis, ingerunt Salvatori salvandos, non Pelagio damnandos. Mater quaelibet mulier pietate currens cum parvulo filio dicit: Baptizetur, ut salvetur." *Sermon 183*, 8.12; PL 38, 992.

[44] Augustine, *Sermon 176*, 2; PL 38, 950; cited by St. Thomas twice, *Summa theologiae*, 3, q. 69, a. 6, ad 3m; q. 71, a. 1, ad 2m.

[45]Yves Congar, "Au lecteur," in Karl Delahaye, *Ecclesia mater chez les Pères des trois premiers siècles: Pour un renouvellement de la Pastorale d'aujourd'hui* (Unam Sanctam 46; Paris: du Cerf, 1964) 7-32. This preface to the French translation of the work is dated 3 September 1963. Reading it, one feels that after the drama of the first session of the Second Vatican Council, Congar was expressing a feeling of liberation, and of vindication. An English version can be found as "Mother Church," in Joseph Ratzinger, *et al.*; *The Church Today* (Cork: Mercier Press, 1967).

were the living stones of which it was constructed.
In other cities, he says, the fabric of the buildings
is one thing, those who inhabit them another; but
in the case of the Church, "this city is built out of
its citizens; its stones are its citizens, for these stones
are living."[46] Developing the same theme in another
sermon, he asks:

> What does it mean, "Be built up as living stones"?
> You are alive if you believe, and if you believe,
> you are being made into the temple of God …
> That city is now being built, therefore. Stones
> are being cut from the mountains by the hands
> of those who are preaching the truth; they are
> being squared so that they may enter into the
> eternal structure. Many stones are still in the
> hands of the builder; let them not fall from his
> hands so that they can be finished and built into
> the structure of the temple.[47]

A MODERN VARIANT

In outlining what a pastoral program might be that
would explore today the implications of the motherhood of the whole Church, Congar said that one
key would be that people be clear about what they
mean by the word "Church," and he used a scho-
lastic Latin question to urge the point: "*Pro quo
supponit Ecclesia?*" What does the word "Church"

[46] Augustine, *En. in Ps. 86*, 3; PL 37, 1103.
[47] Augustine, *En. in Ps. 121*, 4; PL 37, 1620-21.

refer to?[48] In a work written after the Council that took up the question of the relationship between salvation and liberation, Congar devoted a first section to the notion of the Church as "sacrament of salvation." After discussing the notion at the two Vatican Councils, its roots in the Bible and the tradition, and modern efforts to develop it systematically, he added a chapter that not many theologians would have written, entitled "Who is the sacrament of salvation?" Everyone will answer, he begins, "The Church is," but he has the same question to ask, "But what does this word cover? '*Pro quo supponit*,' what lies beneath it?"[49]

If the metaphor of the Church's motherhood directly concerns the birth and nurturing of Christians within the Church, the idea of the Church as the sacrament of salvation looks also to what the Church can contribute to the healing and liberation of mankind. As with the ancient metaphor, Congar insisted that the chief bearer of this responsibility to the world is the whole People of God, the whole community. The tasks it involves are as diverse as what is required wherever human beings suffer want, exploitation, oppression, discrimination, violence, and they are undertaken by individuals acting for Christ's sake, in manners great and small, nursing the ill, teaching people to read and write,

[48] Congar, "Au lecteur," *Ecclesia Mater* 15-16.

[49] Yves Congar, *Un peuple messianique* 75.

defending migrant workers, running soup kitchens – we could multiply the examples that could be given. Such activities embody what it means for the Church to be a sacrament of salvation, a sign and instrument of salvation. The theological notion refers to a concrete reality, Christian individuals and communities.

Sed in quibus?

St. Augustine had asked Congar's question long before. He was preaching one day on Psalm 127, in praise of those who walk in the ways of the Lord. One of the blessings such a person will receive is a happy family life: "Your wife like a fruitful vine on the sides of your house, your children like olive plantings round your table." Augustine takes this verse as addressed to Christ, and so the wife in question here must be Christ's Church. "And his wife, the Church," he immediately clarifies, "is ourselves." But as for this wife's being a "fruitful vine," Augustine asks: "In whom is this vine fruitful?" And he gives the reason he asks: "We see many barren people within these walls; we see many come within them drunk, many who are money-lenders to slave-dealers, others who consult soothsayers, and those who run to enchanters and enchantresses, when they have a headache." In such people, Augustine insists, the vine is not fruitful; they are more like barren thorns.

If Christ's wife is like a fruitful vine, then, in whom is she fruitful? *Sed in quibus?* he asks again. This vine is said to grow on the sides of the house, and the house consists of people who side with Christ, so the answer must be that it is in those who "cling tightly to Christ" that the Church is a fruitful vine.[50]

Implicit in this argument is Augustine's distinction between the Church as the *communio sacramentorum* and the Church as the *societas sanctorum*.[51] The first refers to the Church described in such biblical images as the field in which both wheat and weeds are growing, the net in which bad fish and good are being hauled, the threshing floor where both grain and chaff are found. It is, in other words, the Church here below, gathered under the word of God and born of the sacraments. No one else has so emphasized the mixed character of the Church in her earthly wandering. Only with the judgment of Christ at the end of time will wheat and weeds, the good fish and bad, the grain and the chaff be separated; till then, they are mixed together.

The "fellowship of the holy," on the other hand, refers to those Christians who are living authentic

---

[50] Augustine, *En. in Ps 127*, 11; PL 37, 1684.

[51] See the discussion by Yves Congar, "Introduction générale," in *Oeuvres de saint Augustin: Traités anti-donatistes*, vol. I (Bibliothèque Augustinienne, 28; Bruges: Desclée de Brouwer, 1963) 95-115.

Christian lives. They are the Body of Christ, alive by
his Spirit, united by genuine love. It is the *Ecclesia in
sanctis*, the Church that consists of holy Christians,
who praise God not only with their voices but with
their hearts, not only in appearance but in truth,
who are what the Church ought to be. They are the
true Church in the Augustinian sense for which, as
Congar puts it, "the full truth of its existence ...
is realized when a being becomes what it ought to
be."[52] It is "the ecclesial reality under the angle of
spiritual anthropology insofar as the Church exists,
not as a means of grace or sacrament, ... but as the
totality and the unity of those who live for God,
according to God."[53]

It is important to note that this *societas sanctorum*
is born and can flourish only within the *communio
sacramentorum*. These are not two Churches, one invisible and the other visible, even though only God
can read hearts and know which Christians truly belong to him. Until Christ definitively separates the
good from the bad, good and bad Christians will
coexist within the one Church, which is why Augustine insists, first against the Donatists and then
against the Pelagians, that the Church will be truly
said to be "without spot or wrinkle" only when she
is glorified into the Kingdom of God. Until then,

[52] Ibid. 111.
[53] Ibid. 121, with reference to the relation between the
civitas Dei and the Church.

the Apostle warns us, "if we say that have no sin, we delude ourselves, and the truth is not in us" (1 Jn 1:8); until then, every day, as the Lord commanded her, the whole Church must pray, "Forgive us our trespasses." Augustine put it very neatly: "As long as the holy Church has [sinful] members, she is not without stain and wrinkle."[54]

This paradoxical mixture – holy Church is not without stain and wrinkle – expresses the condition of the Church here and now. The one Church is the community of those who gather under the authority of the Scriptures and by the power of the sacraments; but the Church is what the Church should be only in good, holy Christians. It might be said that the whole purpose of Augustine's preaching was to make the *communio sacramentorum* the *societas sanctorum*.[55]

[54] Augustine, *De continentia*, 25; PL 40, 366. In a sermon against Pelagians, Augustine imagines a dialogue with Pelagians who argue that the Church even now is without spot or wrinkle. Getting them to admit that they themselves are sinners, he replies: "You are Christians; you have been baptized; you are believers; you are members of the Church; and you have spots and wrinkles? How, then, is the Church of this time without spot and wrinkle, since you are the spot and wrinkle?" *Sermon 181*, 3.3; PL 38, 980.

[55] That is why one cannot understand Augustine's ecclesiology without studying his sermons, as is made clear in the wonderful work by Pasquale Borgomeo, *L'Église de ce*

A Precarious Achievement?

Some such distinction is surely necessary in ecclesiology unless one mistakes descriptions of the
ideal with descriptions of the real, assumes that the
ideal is always realized, or separates the two, giv-
ing real hypostasized existence to holy Church over
and above her sinful members. I agree that ecclesiology should have a prescriptive dimension, describing what the Church ought to be in response
to the word and grace of God that bring her into
existence; in fact, I think ecclesiology ought to be
a heuristics of the self-realization of the Church.
But, as Lonergan remarked in a comment directly
relevant, one has to distinguish between religious
conversion as it is described or defined and as it is
realized. What is true of an individual is also true of
the community of believers; their conversion, their
holiness, their authenticity, "is always a withdrawal
from inauthenticity, and the withdrawal is never
complete and always precarious."[56] On this view,
that is, if measured by the criteria that define the *so-*

---

temps dans la prédication de saint Augustin (Paris: Études
Augustiniennes, 1972). That Augustine's preaching was
an effort to make the Church come to be is the convinc-
ing argument of Michael C. McCarthy, "An Ecclesiology
of Groaning: Augustine, the Psalms, and the Making of
the Church," *Theological Studies* 66 (2005) 23-48.
[56] Lonergan, *Method in Theology* 283-84.

cietas sanctorum, the Church is always a precarious achievement. The light of the word of God and the power of his grace are not in doubt, but there are and always will be great differences in the degree to which they are received, appropriated, and lived by individuals and in communities.

The point is obscured when, for example, the question of the holiness of the Church is met by saying that she is unchangeably holy in the means of grace she ministers, but remains sinful in the lives of her members. Louis Bouyer found this answer too facile. The questions arise immediately: what would the Church's "objective holiness" be unless translated into the subjective holiness of her members? And, on the other hand, since the means of grace are ministered by human beings, how can they not be affected by their sins?

To address the question Bouyer distinguished how the divine and the human intertwine in the three areas of pastoral ministry. In the sacraments, the divine element is at its strongest, but their *ex opere operato* effectiveness is owed exclusively to Christ and is known only by pure faith. The human is the perceptible external action. In preaching, the human element is greater, and the grace communicated proportionate to the intelligence and skills of the preacher and to the maturity of those who hear him. Finally, the place of the human, the all-too-human, is greatest in the area of pastoral leadership.

Despite the assistance of the Spirit in this role as much as in the other two, it remains that "there are no errors of judgment, at any level of leadership, there are no sins, individual or collective, in the exercise of authority or pastoral responsibility, that pastors cannot commit. Our only certitude is that the faults of the human instruments of Christ's reign, however serious or numerous, can never destroy the Church." On the other hand, Christ feeds his Church through these human ministers when they have effective love for Christ and nourish the faith of the Church and help believers exercise their faith as charity.[57]

Bouyer's reflections are as concrete as Augustine's were: holy as the Church is in virtue of God's gifts, she exists and acts only in and as a community that very imperfectly lives by their light and power. There is nothing automatic or mechanical about her self-realization. Christ is always at work in her sacraments, yes, and the promise of the Spirit's assistance may be trusted. But how broadly and how deeply Christ and his Spirit effect salvation will always be determined and displayed by the degree of holiness lived within the community of believers.

---

[57] Louis Bouyer, *L'Église de Dieu: Corps du Christ et Temple de l'Esprit* (Paris: Du Cerf, 1970) 613-15; the English translation of the corresponding pages, *The Church of God*, 499-501, is very poor and at times incorrect.

There are degrees, in other words, in the self-realization of the Church.

Earlier I promised to return to the statement in *Lumen gentium* 8, that the Church of Christ "subsists in" the Catholic Church. I believe that the question of the holiness of the Church is, or at least ought to be, a part of the discussion of what this phrase means and does not mean. But before addressing the matter directly, it may prove useful to see what has happened to the discussion of holiness in the Church since St. Thomas Aquinas, following St. Augustine, addressed the matter.

St. Thomas Aquinas on the Holiness of the Church

When, in his lectures on the Creed, St. Thomas Aquinas turned to the article on the Church, he began by taking the word in our sense as the *congregatio fidelium*. "The Church," he said, "is the same thing as an assembly. Holy Church, then, is the same thing as the assembly of believers, and any Christian is like a member of that Church." His treatment of what he called the four characteristics (*conditiones*) of the Church, one immediately sees, will be concrete: he will be talking about the assembly of Christian believers.

That the Church is holy he explains by first contrasting it with another assembly of which the Scriptures speak, the *congregatio malignantium*, assembly of the wicked (Ps 25:5). Christ's Church instead is holy, a claim Thomas supports by citing St Paul: "God's temple is holy, which you are" (1 Cor 3:17). This is why the Creed says that the Church is holy.

To explain this holiness, Aquinas offers this programmatic statement: "The believers of this assembly are made holy (*sanctificantur*) in three ways."[58] In other words, he will explain how the Church is holy by explaining how Christians are holy. For each of these ways, St. Thomas supplies biblical texts in support. His four explanations exploit a comparison with the consecration of a physical church. First, when a church is being consecrated, it is materially washed; so also "believers have been washed in the blood of the Lamb" (Apoc 1:5; Heb 13:12). Second, just as a church is anointed, "believers are anointed with a spiritual anointing in order to be made holy; otherwise they would not be Christians. 'Christ' means 'Anointed One.' Now this anointing is the grace of the Holy Spirit" (2 Cor 1:21; 1 Cor 6:11). Third, "because of the indwelling of the Trinity, for wherever God dwells, that place is holy" (Gen 28:16; Ps 92:5). Fourth, because God's name is invoked in or by the Church (Jer 14:9). Having set out these four reasons why the Church is called holy, St. Thomas concludes with an exhorta-

---

[58] He actually gives four ways; it is good to know that Aquinas could nod off, too.

tion: "We must beware, then, lest after having been made holy by such means we defile by sin our soul, which is the temple of God" (1 Cor 3:17).

A couple of things are notable about Aquinas's argument. First, it does not give holiness a primarily moral meaning, to refer to the state of our souls. The Church is holy because of what God has done: he has washed and anointed her; he dwells within her; his name has been called down upon her. Although Aquinas certainly believed that "the Church is never without people living in grace,"[59] it was not, or at least it was not first of all, because of them that he thought the Church holy. The Church is holy by the act and gift of God. Moral considerations enter only at the end, when the imperative that should flow from the powerful indicative statements are drawn out: we are to be holy because we have been made holy. Even apart from the texts cited by Thomas, one can see how biblical this notion of holiness is.

Second, there is the great concreteness of this treatment. Thomas does not refer to some Church that is apart from her members, whose holiness might be contrasted with their unholiness. The Church is holy because the believers of whom she

[59] "Ecclesia nunquam destituitur existentibus in gratia; unde peccantibus quibusdam, alii in gratiam a domino advocantur"; Aquinas: *Super Sent.*, lib. 1, d. 40 q. 3 a. 1 ad 2

consists have been made holy; one is even tempted to say that she is holy insofar as they have been made holy. It was because he approached the Church so concretely that Aquinas could agree with Augustine that "being 'without spot or wrinkle,' is the final goal to which we are being drawn by the passion of Christ. This will be the case, therefore, when we reach our homeland, but not while we are still on the journey during which 'if we say that we do not have sin, we deceive ourselves' (1 Jn 1:8)."[60]

This concrete biblical approach was still being urged for centuries after Aquinas; it is strongly stated and defended, for example, in the Catechism of the Council of Trent.[61] More recently, however,

---

[60] Aquinas, *Summa theologiae*, 3, q. 8, a. 3, ad 2m.

[61] "No one should be surprised that the Church, although it contains many sinners, is called holy. For as those who profess any art, even though they depart from its rules, are still called artists, so in like manner believers, although offending in many things and failing in the commitments to which they had pledged themselves, are still called holy, because they have been made the people of God and have consecrated themselves to Christ by faith and Baptism. That is why St. Paul calls the Corinthians sanctified and holy, even though it is clear that among them there were some whom he severely rebuked as fleshly and with even more serious names." *The Catechism by Decree of the Holy Council of Trent* (Rome: Propaganda Press, 1839), I, 202-205 – my translation.

distinctions have been made that one will not find in Augustine and Aquinas. One that seems to enjoy a certain favor at the moment is the formula of Charles Journet: "The Church is without sin but not without sinners."[62] Journet, along with his close friend Jacques Maritain, was of the view that the Church has a personhood of her own distinct from the persons of her members; to speak of the Church in terms of her members is to use a restricted, even an impoverished, sense of the term.[63] It is the Church in the full sense that is unfailingly united to Christ as Body to Head, that is indefectibly holy in her being and in her activity. To her belong individual Christians in virtue of what is holy in them, of what lives by supernatural charity; by what is unholy in them, however, they do not belong to the holy Church. They may be said to be members of the Church, but the sin is theirs and not the Church's. In that sense it can be said that the Church is without sin but not without sinners.

This distinction was so taken for granted by Journet that it permitted him, quite unconsciously, I

[62] See a collection of his papers in Charles Journet, *L'Église sainte mais non sans pécheurs* (Paris: Éd. Parole et Silence, 1999).

[63] See Charles Journet, "On Three Ways of Defining the Word 'Church' and on the Corresponding Ways of Assigning her Causes," in *The Church of the Word Incarnate: vol. I: The Apostolic Hierarchy* 45-59.

suspect, to attribute it to Aquinas. Here is Journet's paraphrase of the passage, cited above, in which St. Thomas spoke of believers being washed.

> The Church is holy, wrote St. Thomas, because she washes believers in the blood of Christ, as is said in the Apocalypse, "He loved us; he washed our sins in his blood, and he has made us kings and priests for God and his Father," and in Hebrews: "Jesus, having to sanctify the people by his blood, suffered outside the gate."[64]

What in the biblical texts and in Aquinas's commentary is the work of Christ in his saving passion, Journet attributes to the Church in her sanctifying, sacramental role, and the Church which Aquinas had identified with believers as the recipients of that great act of redemption has now been set over and against believers to the point that it is now the Church that is said to wash believers clean in the blood of the Lamb.

WHERE IS THE CHURCH TO BE FOUND?

I end by discussing the relevance of these considerations to the question recently addressed by the Congregation for the Doctrine of the Faith in its document "Responses to Some Questions regarding Certain Aspects of the Doctrine of the Church" [CDF] (June 29, 2007). As you may know, the

[64] Journet, *L'Église sainte mais non sans pécheurs* 50.

Congregation maintained in the text that the Second Vatican Council had not changed Catholic doctrine on the Church but had rather "developed, deepened and more fully explained it." In particular, it maintained that the Council's use in *Lumen gentium* 8 of the verb "subsists in," in place of an earlier simple "is," did not represent a change from the Catholic Church's claim to be the one true Church. The verb "subsists in" could be used only of the Roman Catholic Church. While Orthodox communities could properly be called Churches, they lack an inner constitutive principle, communion with the Catholic Church. Protestant communities, on the other hand, because they lack "apostolic succession in the sacrament of Orders" and "have not preserved the genuine and integral substance of the Eucharistic Mystery, cannot, according to Catholic doctrine, be called 'Churches' in the proper sense."

The CDF statement is correct that the Council was not surrendering the unique claims that the Catholic Church has traditionally made about herself. The Doctrinal Commission explained to the Council Fathers the purpose of the eighth paragraph of *Lumen gentium*:

> The *intention* is to show that the Church, whose intimate and mysterious nature which forever unites it with Christ and his work has been described, here on earth is concretely found [*concrete invenitur*] in the Catholic Church. While

this empirical Church reveals the mystery, it does not do so without shadows until it is brought to full light, just as Christ the Lord came to his glory by emptying himself. Thus is avoided the impression that the description of the Church which the Council presents is merely idealistic and unreal.

A clearer *subdivision* is thus offered, which successively deals with the following:

a) The mystery of the Church is present [*adest*] and is manifested *in a concrete society*. The visible assembly and the spiritual element *are not two realities*, but one complex reality, comprising divine and human elements, the means of salvation and the fruits of salvation. And this is illustrated by analogy with the Incarnate Word.

b) The Church is *one*, and here on earth is present [*adest*] in the Catholic Church, although ecclesial elements are found outside it.

c) The manifestation of the mystery in the Catholic Church occurs at once *in power and in weakness*, that is also in a condition of poverty and persecution, of sin and purification, so that the Church is like Christ, although he was without sin. Following the desires of the Fathers, the theme of poverty is somewhat developed.

d) The Church overcomes all these difficulties *by the power of Christ and love* by which it reveals the mystery, even though under shadows, until it comes to full light.[65]

---

[65] *Acta Synodalia*, III/I, 176.

When the Doctrinal Commission came to the text in which the word "is" [*est*] is replaced by the words "subsists in" [*subsistit in*], it explained the change in this way:

> Some words are changed: in place of "is" the text says "subsists in" so that the expression may better accord with the affirmation about ecclesial elements that are present [*adsunt*] elsewhere.[66]

This alteration did not please all the bishops, some of whom proposed amendments. The Doctrinal Commission summarized them and responded to them:

> Nineteen Fathers propose: "subsists *integrally* in the Catholic Church." Twenty-five others want to add: "subsists *by divine right.*" Another thirteen Fathers want to write "is" in place of "subsists in." One Father proposes "*consists*" instead of "*subsists.*" Two tendencies are clearly manifest here, one which would somewhat extend the view, while the other would like to restrict it. The Doctrinal Commission had already had a lengthy discussion of the matter and then chose the words "subsists in," a solution with which everyone present agreed. As for adding "*integrally,*" see the text in # 14. As for adding "*by divine right,*" it is clear from the paragraph's context, that the text is speaking about Christ's

---

[66] *Acta Synodalia*, III,I, 177.

institution. *The response* is: The agreed upon text
should be kept.[67]

Surprisingly, these clarifications of the Doctrinal
Commission are not cited in the recent CDF document, which instead offers several telling comments
from the same Commission related to the Decree
on Ecumenism (*Unitatis redintegratio*). On the other hand, the recent text does offer a close paraphrase
when it says that "subsists in" was chosen in order
more clearly to bring out "the fact that there are
'numerous elements of sanctification and of truth'
that are found outside her structure."

A more balanced and ecumenically more sensi-
tive document would have resulted had the CDF
followed the Doctrinal Commission's lead and
presented what the Council said about ecclesial
elements found outside the Catholic Church; this
would also have made it possible to present what the
Council was and was not claiming by the use of the
verb "subsists in."[68] There are several texts in which
the Council describes the constitutive elements of
the Church. The general statement about "numerous elements of sanctification and truth" (*Lumen*

[67] *Acta Synodalia,*. III/VI, 81.

[68] I have found no evidence that in choosing the verb
"subsists in," the Doctrinal Commission had philosophical considerations in mind, as the CDF seems to imply.
It does not seem that the verb is used here with any more

gentium 8) is clarified and amplified in three other passages.

First, in *Lumen gentium* 14, the Council defined "full incorporation" into the society of the Church, a phrase that the Council preferred to the language of "membership."

> Those persons are fully incorporated into the society of the Church who, possessing the Spirit of Christ, accept all the means of salvation given to the Church along with its entire organization [*ordinatio*] and who, by the bonds constituted by the profession of faith, the sacraments, ecclesiastical government, and communion, are joined in the visible structure of the Church to Christ, who rules it through the Supreme Pontiff and the bishops.

The statement is important because full incorporation gives some clues as to what the constitutive elements of the Church are. We can make, then, a first list:

the Spirit of Christ	the means of salvation
organization	profession of faith
sacraments	ecclesiastical government
communion	the visible structure

precision than it is in other conciliar statements (UR 4, 13, DH 1; GS 10; in 3, it refers to God), where its meaning seems to be "continues to exist." In any case, the key to the meaning is not the word itself but its use in a sentence.

One will note that by these criteria, only Roman Catholics can be fully incorporated into the society of the Church, since only they acknowledge the authority of the pope, but that not all Roman Catholics are fully incorporated, since many of them do not have the Spirit of Christ.

In the next paragraph (*Lumen gentium* 15), the Council discusses lesser degrees of communion when it speaks about the links between the Catholic Church and non-Catholic Christian *individuals*. Here can be found another list of elements:

Sacred Scripture	religious zeal
loving faith in God & Christ	baptism
union with Christ	other sacraments
the episcopate	the Eucharist
devotion to Mary	prayer & spiritual blessings
true union in the Spirit	the Spirit's gifts & graces
the Spirit's sanctifying power	

But the strongest statement is found in *Unitatis redintegratio* #3, where the Council discusses the relationship between the Catholic Church and other Christian *communities*:

> Some, even very many, of the most significant elements and endowments that together go to build up and to give life to the Church itself can exist outside the visible boundaries of the Catholic Church: the written Word of God, the life of grace, faith, hope, and charity, with

other inner gifts of the Holy Spirit, as well as visible elements.

Not a few of the sacred actions of the Christian religion are also carried out among the brethren separated from us, actions which in various ways according to the different conditions of each Church or Community, without a doubt can really generate the life of Christ and must be said to be able to open the way to the communion of salvation.

For that reason these separated Churches and Communities, even if we believe that they suffer from lacks [*defectus*], are by no means deprived of meaning and weight in the mystery of salvation. For Christ does not refuse to use them as means of salvation whose power derives from that fullness of grace and truth which has been entrusted to the Catholic Church.

Anyone of a certain age, with a memory of how frosty, to put it very mildly, relations were between Catholics and non-Catholic Christians as late as the 1950s, will recognize what extraordinary statements these are. Outside the Catholic Church, in Christian individuals and in their communities and Churches, can be found the primary elements that describe the inner life of the Church: justifying and sanctifying grace; faith, hope, and love; communion in the Holy Spirit. Even some of the sacraments may be found in some of the communities, where they can generate the life of Christ and medi-

ate salvation. Lutherans, to illustrate, can be saved
not in spite of being Lutherans, but because their
communities have preserved so many of the constitutive and animating elements of the Church.

Having described in such strong terms what is
present in these other communities, the Council
then made its statement about what it believes to
be unique about the Roman Catholic Church:

> But the brethren separated from us, whether as
> individuals or as Communities and Churches, do
> not enjoy that unity which Jesus Christ wished
> to bestow on all those whom he has regenerated
> and vivified together into one body and into a
> new life, that unity which the Sacred Scriptures
> and the Church's ancient Tradition profess. For
> it is through the Catholic Church of Christ
> alone, which is the universal help towards salva-
> tion, that the fullness of the means of salvation
> can be attained. It was to the apostolic College
> alone, with Peter as its head, that we believe that
> the Lord entrusted all the blessings of the New
> Covenant in order to establish on earth one
> Body of Christ into which all those should be
> fully incorporated who in any way belong to the
> People of God. This people, during its earthly
> pilgrimage, although in its members still liable
> to sin, grows in Christ and is being gently guided
> in accord with God's mysterious counsels until
> it comes joyfully to the entire fullness of eternal
> glory in the heavenly Jerusalem.

This passage provides the best explanation of the unique claim that the Roman Catholic Church makes about itself and, thereby, I believe, sets out what "subsists in" means in *Lumen gentium* 8. The key sentence is: "it is through the Catholic Church alone that the fullness of the means of salvation can be attained." This is not a claim that the Catholic Church alone possesses the truth and grace of Christ; it is not a claim that it is holier than other Churches or communities. It is a claim about the "means of salvation," that is, institutions, ordinances, etc., with which God has blessed the Church for the sake of the salvation of its members. If these can be set out in terms of the ancient pillars of the Catholic form of the Church, they would include: the rule of apostolic faith (the Creed); the canon of apostolic Scriptures; the form of apostolic worship (sacraments); and the structure of apostolic ministry. To take some examples: Catholics believe that the canon of the Scriptures includes texts that Protestants do not receive, that there are seven sacraments willed by Christ, that the normative ministry includes that of the Bishop of Rome as minister of catholic unity. The Catholic Church regards these as divinely willed elements of the Church, and since other Christian Churches or communities lack one of more of them,[69] the Council can say that the

---

[69] This is what the Council meant when it spoke of "*defectus*" in other Christian Churches or communities

fullness of these means of salvation is found in the Catholic Church alone.

The Council's statement is considering the Church in its divinely instituted elements as the sacrament, instrument, and sign of salvation. It is focusing on the instrumental aspect, the elements through which Christ and his Spirit continue to work through the Church. There is, of course, a certain abstraction to the description, perhaps necessarily so. The formal elements that make up the Church may be described or defined; but, as Bouyer pointed out, these elements – creed, canon, sacraments, ministry – do not effect the Church except as enacted by the men and women who make up the Church. The creed and the canon of the Scriptures are only black marks on white paper unless appropriated by believers; the sacraments exist only as and when being celebrated; the apostolic ministry is only active in the men who undertake it. To adapt a point made earlier: the *Ecclesia convocans* is always the *Ecclesia convocata*: it is always the Church that has resulted from the communication of the Gospel that now communicates the Gospel.

This means, however, that while "the fullness of grace and truth" may have been entrusted to the Catholic Church, the degree to which they are re-

---

(*Unitatis Redintegratio* 3). "Lacks" is a better translation than "defects" or "wounds."

ceived and lived can vary greatly. The Council acknowledged this when it spoke of the Church as "at once holy and always in need of purification" and as having continually to pursue repentance and renewal (*Lumen gentium* 8). The gifts of God account for the holiness of the Church; the failure to realize them fully accounts for her constant need of purification.[70]

---

[70] At the beginning of his literal interpretation of Genesis, Augustine gave a brief summary of the Catholic faith which includes the belief that "the Holy Spirit was given to those who believe in him, and that Mother Church was established by him; she is called 'catholic' because she is complete in every respect, is lacking in nothing (*in nullo claudicat*), and is spread throughout the world." *De genesi ad litteram, imperfectus liber*, I, 4; PL 34, 221-22. The Latin verb *claudicare* means literally "to be lame, to limp," but it has an applied meaning of "to lack, be defective," and it is the latter that is surely meant here: the Catholic Church has all it should have. This, I take it, is what the CDF wished to say about the Catholic Church. But Augustine did not hesitate to use the associated adjective *claudus*, lame, limping, to describe the Church as he knew it. Interpreting the account of Jacob's wrestling with the angel and coming away both blessed and limping, Augustine saw him as a figure of the Church because of the presence in her of evil Christians. "The Church limps now (*Modo clauda est Ecclesia*); she puts one foot down strongly, but her other foot is weak" *Sermon 5*, 9; PL 38, 59.

We are brought back, then, to the criteria that
constitute "full incorporation" into the Church as
described in *Lumen gentium* 14. The list of tradi-
tional external criteria – profession of the faith, sacramental communion, acknowledgment of authority – is preceded by three simple words, *Spiritum
Christi habentes* (possessing the Spirit of Christ),
that, as Joseph Ratzinger pointed out shortly after
the Council,[71] transform the old question of membership in the Church. Robert Bellarmine thought
it was an advantage of his definition of the Church
that to determine its members no inner virtue was
required so that it was as possible on the basis of
public criteria to identify where the true Church
was as it was to determine where the Republic of
Venice or the Kingdom of France were. This might
have met one way in which the question *de vera
ecclesia* was posed, but it quite ignored another
of its meanings, namely the question where is the
Church truly, that is, authentically present?[72]

By placing a spiritual criterion in the first place,
Ratzinger argued, the Council raised the ques-

[71] Joseph Ratzinger, "Theologische Aufgaben und Fragen
bei der Begegnung lutherischer und katholischer Theol-
ogie nach dem Konzil," in *Das neue Volk Gottes: Entwürfe
zur Ekklesiologie* (Düsseldorf: Patmos, 1969) 225-45,
esp. 242-45; for his early interpretation of the "*subsistit
in*" formula and its significance, see pp. 235-37.
[72] See Dianich, *Ecclesiologia* 23-26.

tion of "holiness as an essential requirement of the Church." He agreed with a statement of Hans Urs von Balthasar that "the Church is most fully present where faith, hope and love, selflessness and support of others are found most fully."[73] From Balthasar he also borrowed a distinction between the Church's official heights and her inner heights; the latter existing "where she is most herself, that is, where holiness, where conformity to Christ, are most present. The inner height of the Church can, therefore, reach far beyond her institutional boundaries." This recognition, Ratzinger went on, overcomes the narrowness with which disputes over Church membership and over the ecclesial character of other Churches were carried out, that is, with a focus on the order of means. As indispensable as these are, they are not the entire essence of the Church. If they must not be separated, neither do they entirely coincide, and there could be more of the Church's inner reality where there is less of its outer reality, and vice-versa.[74]

[73] Ratzinger cited from Balthasar's essay, "Who is the Church?" 172.

[74] The same conclusion was reached by Hermann Josef Pottmeyer, "Die Frage nach der wahren Kirche," in *Handbuch der Fundamental-theologie*, 3, Traktat Kirche, ed. Hermann Josef Pottmeyer and Max Seckler (Frieburg: Herder, 1986), 212-41. The Italian Theological Association published an entire volume on love as a constitutive

These are ecumenical implications discerned in the conciliar text by one who participated in its elaboration; one could wish that they had been developed in the CDF's latest document, as indeed in its earlier Letter *Communionis notio*. It was content with only one way of asking the question about "the one true Church," and to it it gave the answer that, as Catholics believe, only in the Catholic Church are "the fullness of the means of salvation" to be found. But there is another way of asking where the true Church is that cannot be answered so neatly, even by Catholics, because the question then is "Where is the authentic Church?" This is what Augustine was asking: "*Sed in quibus?*" "In whom," that is, "in what men and women, in what communities, is the Church authentically realized?" In the end, it is in individual Christians and in their local communities and Churches, in the varied circumstances of time and place, before the differing challenges of their historical moments, that the most telling answer will be found to my question: "Who are the Church?"

---

principle of the Church: *De caritate Ecclesia: Il principio "amore" e la chiesa* (Padova: Ed. Messaggero, 1987); see in particular the introductory essay by Severino Dianich, "'De caritate Ecclesia': Introduzione ad un tema inconsueto," pp. 27-107.

1977 *Truth Beyond Relativism:*
Karl Mannheim's Sociology of Knowledge
Gregory Baum

1978 *A Theology of 'Uncreated Energies'*
George A. Maloney, S.J.

1980 *Method in Theology: An Organon for Our*
Time
Frederick E. Crowe, S.J.

1981 *Catholics in the Promised Land of the*
Saints
James Hennesey, S.J.

1982 *Whose Experience Counts in Theological*
Reflection?
Monika Hellwig

1983 *The Theology and Setting of Discipleship*
in the
Gospel of Mark
John R. Donahue, S.J.

1984 *Should War Be Eliminated?*
Philosophical and Theological Investigations
Stanley Hauerwas

1990 *Is Mark's Gospel a Life of Jesus?*
The Question of Genre
Adela Yarbro Collins

1991 *Faith, History and Cultures:*
Stability and Change in Church Teachings
Walter H. Principe, C.S.B.

1992 *Universe and Creed*
Stanley L. Jaki

1993 *The Resurrection of Jesus Christ:*
Some Contemporary Issues
Gerald G. O'Collins, S.J.

1994 *Seeking God in Contemporary Culture*
Most Reverend Rembert G. Weakland,
O.S.B.

1995 *The Book of Proverbs and Our Search for*
Wisdom
Richard J. Clifford, S.J.

1996 *Orthodox and Catholic Sister Churches:*
East Is West and West Is East
Michael A. Fahey, S.J.

About the Père Marquette Lecture Series

The Annual Père Marquette Lecture Series began at Marquette University in the Spring of 1969. Ideal for classroom use, library additions, or private collections, the Père Marquette Lecture Series has received international acceptance by scholars, universities, and libraries. Hardbound in blue cloth with gold stamped covers. Uniform style and price ($15 each). Some reprints with soft covers. Regular reprinting keeps all volumes available. Ordering information (purchase orders, checks, and major credit cards accepted):

Marquette University Press
Order Toll-Free (800) 247-6553
fax: (419) 281 6883

Order directly online: www.marquette.edu/mupress/

Editorial Address:

Dr. Andrew Tallon, Director
Marquette University Press
Box 3141
Milwaukee WI 53201-3141

phone:	(414) 288-1564
fax:	(414) 288-7813
email:	andrew.tallon@marquette.edu
web:	www.marquette.edu/mupress/